Confessio
of a Wall

CW00421436

Confessions of a Wallflower

Juansen Dizon

For my mom who helped me with my anxiety and depression.
And to all my readers online. Especially those who suffers from
mental illness like me.
I love you all very much.

The 19-year-old Juansen Dizon who wrote and compiled this poetry collection no longer exists.

The 19-year-old Juansen Dizon hopes that this book will change him.

Contents

The
Depression

I feel therefore I love.

The Bittersweet Feeling

Sigh, the bittersweet feeling of being in love and being alive both at the same time.

Love

I could never grasp the true meaning of love, but it would forever be the sad beat of my heart.

Love is.
Love is.
Love is.

Sad

I feel sad for I have lost all meaning of love through all my suffering and I am trying to find it there.

Depression

Depression isn't like the weather, and the people who have it aren't like skies. The sadness, the anxiety, and the hopelessness are constant. It doesn't come and go like most people think it does.

The best thing a person can do for someone with depression is to accept that it frequently rains in their world. To be their love, warmth, and light when there seems to be no light at the end of the tunnel.

Fragile Flower

I am a soft person
but only to myself.

I am too fragile for
this world. I am a fragile
flower.

And I think I need to
be surrounded by a thousand
suns to grow.

I need to be the warm center
of this world.

Romantic

I am both self-destructive and self-loving.
Both seem very romantic to me.

Discovery

Find love and healing in your sadness.

Cancer

Depression is like cancer for the soul.
It eats it up, and it starts slow, and unknowingly so.

Recovery

The only person I'm recovering from is myself.

Life

Life is a healing process. There is no cure for it.
There is no key to permanent happiness only to temporary
happiness. Trust the process. And there you will find
natural happiness.

Fragile

Be gentle
with your
sadness.

It is preparing
you for your
happiness.

Double-Edged Sword

Sadness is both a curse and a blessing.
It has the power to heal, and it has the power to kill.

The Healing Power of Sadness

Sadness is my power.

I heal people's wounds with it. I heal my own wounds with it. I teach people how to wield it but more sadly—people dismiss it for pessimism or nihilism, and I can't really blame them for telling me that I should be more positive and that I should choose to be happy and that I should avoid thoughts that make me sad and think of positive thoughts instead.

The thing is—sadness cannot be buried alive with positive thoughts. Positive thoughts will only serve as a fertilizer to the sadness that is planted deep beneath a person's heart. And when sadness is neglected for a long period of time— it could grow into anger and irritation.

And that's the reason why some people experience burnout in life because we live in a society that romanticizes over exhaustion and over positive thinking that we forget that expressing our sadness to the people we love in life is the key to our total well-being which is much better than temporary happiness that is caused by sadness suppressing self-affirmations that are a common practice these days.

So rather than using over exhaustion to improve ourselves why don't we give self-care and self-love a chance by being more truthful in what we truly feel.

And then find the energy we need in whatever we do in life from the comfort and sympathy of the people we love in times of sadness and happiness.

And then we can reciprocate by spending quality time with the people we love whether they're happy or sad. Because the human emotion is like a piano composed of white and black keys. And the black keys creates beautiful music too when combined with the white keys.

In conclusion, the key to successful well-being is being emotionally literate. And it all starts by accepting the emotions that we're truly feeling. After all the truth will always set us free.

Power

You have the power to recreate yourself from your brokenness.

Self-Forgiveness

Forgive yourself of your past. Forgive yourself for loving the wrong people. Forgive yourself for being the wrong person to be loved by someone you've hurt in the past.

Forgive yourself because you've learned that you can never forget who you were in the past, but you can always remember who you are in the future. A person filled with love and forgiveness to others and to oneself. A person who always has the power to start again.

Melancholy Warrior

You will sad your way out of life.
You will cry.
You will scream.

And when the sadness is over.
You will try.
You will dream.

Self-Healing

If you want healing, love your sadness. If you want peace, love your loneliness. If you want death, love your sorrow.

Finch

I am a bird.
I am flight.
I am panic.
I am anxiety.
I am free and lonely
in my blue sky of sadness.

Therapy

My psychiatrist told me that I should expose myself to social situations more to reduce my social anxiety. And I think she's right. But it's funny because the only way to overcome my social anxiety is by more anxiety. And I think that's life for everyone in this world. A combination of fight and flight. Like taking two steps forward and taking one step back. Except sometimes I am more flight than fight.

The Thirteen Rules of My Life:

1. I am allowed to cry.
2. I am required to try.
3. I am allowed to give up.
4. I am required to get back up.
5. I am not allowed to love without loving myself first.
6. I am required to say sorry to the people I've done wrong.
7. I am required to forgive.
8. I am allowed to move on.
9. I am allowed to be happy.
10. I am allowed to do the work I love.
11. I am required to do my best in the work I love.
12. I am required to live.
13. I am not allowed to kill myself.

Season

You need to realize that the sadness that you are feeling right now will not be permanent. But I also need you to realize that the sadness that you're feeling right now will happen again anytime in the future because we live in a world where bad things happen to good people and bad people. But until then I hope you feel okay with the fact that joy will come like how spring comes after winter. But I also hope that you'll feel okay when summer ends. When the crushed leaves of autumn starts falling on you. Just please don't kill yourself. Because I know that someone out there loves you. And that the love that he or she is feeling for you right now is permanent.

Choose Life

I did not kill myself.
I chose to live because
I have so many things to die for.
I am death, and every day I search for life.

November 13, 2016

Today I am not the person whom I thought I was yesterday. Today I am not the person whom I thought I would be tomorrow. Today I am going to start living more outside my own thoughts and reach out to the people whom I love and consider family. Today I am going to stay alive.

The Thing With Feathers

Hope, dear mind.

Dark Places

Hope is created in all the dark places.

ture

Depression and hope share the same reality.

Blue

I cannot really say that I know what it feels like to be broken-hearted even though I've probably experienced it a thousand times. What I can tell you is this. Every heartache and heartbreak is unique. Every teardrop that falls from your eyes has its own unique shape that is similar to a winter's snowflake. Release them. Let them fall. You always have the right to cry. You always have the right to be in sadness until there is no more sadness left to be sad. You always have the right to be happy when you finally stretch up your arms up in the air and feel the happy summer's wind shake your hands and congratulates you on making it to a new day, a new life, a new existence. And that day will be the first day of the rest of your life. You will be reborn into something much more beautiful after an extended period of loneliness. Like how a butterfly hatches from its cocoon and no longer feels blue inside its own shell from the moment it flaps its wings and flies towards the blue sky of tomorrow filled with hope.

Teachers

Depression taught me how to hope.
Anxiety taught me how to fight.
Suicidality taught me how to live.
And poetry taught me how to love.

Teaching

I am teaching every person in my life where
I want to be in their life.

It's the only way I can teach them how much
I love them.

It Gets Worse

You just become more—
Resilient.
Strong.
Brave.
And hopeful.

It's only the hope that gets better.
It's the thing that never dies.
It's the thing with feathers—
That always flies.

Quicksand

Sadness is like being stuck in quicksand. You don't struggle your way out of it. You need to relax and accept that you are sad. You need to cry. You need to admit that you're fucked. Then and only then you have a shot at a silver lining.

anvas

Paint the stars and the moon
back into my night sky and tell
me it is okay to cry without asking
why.

A Hug For Myself

I cried as I placed both of my hands on top of my chest. Feeling the warm tantrum inside it. For all the things it wanted but couldn't. And I whispered, "It's okay. It's okay. It's okay. Let it all out."

Icarus

I wear the crown of
my delusion of grandeur.

To be loved for who
I am, and to rise above the stars.

To touch, to kiss—
the sun.

Flying with my—
Icarus wings.

Falling down the deep blue sea of
sadness, I drown, I burn—

I sing.

Calling

The deep blue sea is calling me, and I must go.
I must drown with the sun.

Insomnia

I spend countless of
early sleepless mornings
alone thinking if I should
end it all.

November 18, 2016

It's sad because there are some nights when I think the next day would be awesome and I just couldn't sleep. And then the next day I wake up and I couldn't because depression has reminded me that sometimes I am as blue as the sky.

Sleepers

I am both the child on the bed
And the monster under the bed.
And both are tired. Both are sleeping.

Ambien

I took a sleeping pill and flew to the stars. Away from my problems.

Rise

I woke up, and nothing inspired me to live.

December 4, 2016

Sometimes I feel like I'm watching myself from the sky, and everything feels so unreal.

Compound

I am made up of
ninety percent anxiety
and ten percent empty.

Sufficient enough
to blast off my sky blue colored city.

Eeyore

When everything falls apart, I still have my dog.

Hope

Every time I finish crying
I wipe my tears away from
my eyes as I look at the sky and
believe in the thing with feathers.

Survival

There are some days in life when you look up the sky, and see the clouds are dark gray. Those kind of days when you feel like life has no meaning, and you are afraid that you're not doing anything about it to give it meaning.

Well sometimes those are the kind of days when making it to the next is what gives life meaning.

The Art of Losing Myself

I am the moon,
and sometimes I shine full in my dark,
and sometimes I shine half in my dark,
and sometimes I am the darkness myself.

Stars

I am waiting for a sign from the stars
if tonight will be the night I'll find peace
beneath the flowers.

Isolation

I am sorry if I disappear for awhile one day.
I am just wandering into my own world when that
happens.

Hermit

I want to live every day alone and not feel lonely.

Oblivion

In my life
there are no rainbows after rains
there are no stars in darkness
only hopelessness
and pains.

October 23, 2016

It has been awhile since I spoke to a friend. I spend most days at home reading books. Just writing all my sorrows away. And it gets dull after awhile. Spending most of my time alone in the dark. Missing the feeling of what it's like to have a social life.

But the sad thing is—I am anxious with the slightest social interaction because I feel like I'm ugly and awkward and boring. And I use thought as an excuse for me not to participate in life because I am afraid to live.

And the truth is—I want to die. But I am afraid of pain. And I use fear as an excuse to continue my existence because I am also afraid to die.

Fake Smiles

I ate so many
fake smiles today,
and it's time to vomit
them all in my room tonight.

Silent

I am silent of my pain because
I am the only one who needs to feel it.

Catharsis

Maybe I am being
punished for the sin
of not loving myself,
and how I thought
sinning was enough
suffering.

Captive

I am held captive by my own thoughts that I think I would end up spending my entire life through excessive introspection.

Hoax

Why do we have comedies? Because life is a tragedy.
Why do we have tragedies? Because life is a joke.

Nothingness

I'm going to die one day. And that fact alone should force me to live my life to the fullest. But I'm the opposite way around. I want to die because I am consistently eaten up by nothingness.

Inferno

I set myself on fire, and no one even cares to watch me burn.

King of the Ashes

I am going to live again.
I am going to build my kingdom on ashes.
I am going to create a better world above the abysses of
my mind.

Atlantis

I am alive in my suicidal mind
trying to breathe through poetry.

My ankles and wrists
are chained to the bottom of the sea
breathing hydrogen.

I am a mermaid lost
at this bottomless sea trying
to find a way out of my mind.

Love is oxygen.

Gray Matter

I treasure my brain so much because despite all the sorrow, pain, and sadness it causes me it still chooses to think of a life filled with joy, healing, and happiness. And best of all it still chooses to live.

Rain

I am like the rain.
Soft, but could leave
you cold.

Blissful, but could drown
an entire city.

November 5, 2016

I'm always sad even in times when I am happy. Is that weird? That I feel everything so deeply that even in happy moments I am sad because I am afraid that I'll never be happy for the same reason because I have already felt it? That I have ruined precious moments in life by feeling too much that those moments just turns into sad memories that I'll always look back to whenever I feel the need to remember what it's like to feel every time I feel absolutely nothing at all.

Alpha

The first thing I saw when
I was born was the sky and
how I felt the rain on my skin.

The Work of Dreams

I am a human being with clinical depression. And I find healing by confessing to the world that I am unwell through sharing my poetry. And it is through sharing my poetry that I realized that healing for me is not a destination but rather a lifelong journey. That life for everyone is not cured, but rather life for everyone is maintained by showing mutual love to each other in the service of performing the work of dreams.

Hangman

Some days
I feel like
a human.

Some days
I feel like
a hangman.

Homo Sapien

Through your endless sorrow
you will find what it means to be completely human.

Human (Noun)

I am human.
I am alpha.
I am happiness.
I am sadness.
I am creator.
I am dreamer.
I am believer.
I am glorious.
I am victorious.
I am loved.

I Am

I think that the two most powerful words in the world are found in the phrase *I am*. I being the subject and am being the link to something that I believe is true about myself. Like *I am* joy because *I am* alive.

Like *I am* sad because *I am* tired because *I am* human.

Like *I am* loved because *I am*.

Human Being

More than my clinical depression and social anxiety.
More than my proses and poetry.
I am in love with the human being me.

I Am Human

No other title can make me feel less than this.
No other title can make me feel more than this.
I am human. Just like everyone else. Any other title
isn't enough to interpret my soul and my whole being.

You Are Not Your Mental Illness

You are your dreams.
You are your hobbies.
You are your natural gifts and talents.
You are your pet's most favorite person in the world.
You are your friend's important friend.
You are your parent's proudness.
You are your humanity.
You are a human being the best human being you can be.

November 23, 2016

I wasn't really good at being a functional human being.
I liked playing video games for at least 12 hours a day.
I couldn't eat. I was too anxious to eat. I would just vomit
it all up. And I couldn't sleep. Then comes school the next
day and my brain would just be stuck somewhere in limbo.
And I masturbated at least two times a day. I just didn't
care. I was too depressed to take care of myself and I just
really wanted to die because it was obvious that I wouldn't
amount to anything and I needed to seek help.

Human Love

Depression is more managed than cured. And there's no greater anti-depressant than human love and connection.

Bullies

All you need to know about the people who tries to inflict pain on you is that they are in severe pain themselves. You may hurt from the things they do to you, but you can always choose to be a spectator rather than a victim.

Empathy

More than I want to be understood,
I want to learn how to understand.

Stigma

It seems so simple when people tell me to be happy without any reason, but it seems so complicated when I tell people that I am sad with a reason.

Mental Health

Your mental health is more important than everything.

September 21, 2016

I must say that the advocacy against mental health stigma is thriving.

We are on the winning side in this constant battle. And that is because of the people who openly and shamelessly post about their mental illness on social media not because they're attention seekers but because they want to prove to society that mental illness is not a made up fairy tale.

So to the girl who posted a picture of how thin she was because of anorexia and how she gained weight now, I am proud that you're eating well now.

To the boy who posted a picture of his scars half a year ago, I am proud that you're not cutting yourself anymore. And that takes a lot of courage and willpower. Well done.

And to everyone who writes, muse, or make poems about mental illness, I am happy that you are alive in this universe because you have a story to tell that may change people's lives forever.

Brothers and sisters. As long as we don't kill ourselves, we will not be oppressed. We will win this war. There is hope.

Willpower

Sometimes it's only the will to stay alive that's necessary to feel something.

True Resilience

It isn't about standing every time we fall.
It's about stumbling into the right place where we know
we can stand again.

eful

And after everything I've been through in my baneful life,
I still want to live.

Your Words

Your words have meaning.
Sometimes it's what gives you healing.
Sometimes it's what makes you get over the feeling.

Partnership

My mind; the poet.
My heart; the sadness.

Disenchanted

It was sadness that made my heart ache to write. It wasn't the sadness that came from the world. It was my own sadness.

Sadness

I am tired of sadness, but sadly that's what sadness does.

Problems

Yes, there might be children starving in Africa and wars going on in the Middle East. But that doesn't make your problem less painful just because it is less tragic than the things that are happening outside your control.

I can't live, I will live.

The
Love

Reveal to me everything you find ugly about yourself, so
I can reveal to you everything I find beautiful about you.

Evening Song

Love is when the night owls go
leafing along the moon's shape.

Their astronomical eyes squinting
perceptibly. Grasping the essence
behind the moon's mercurial
anatomy.

A pulchritude given birth by illumination.

Avant-Garde

To be honest, sometimes I don't know what to write.
I sometimes think that everything great and original has already been written. And I am afraid that my love for you is the only original thought in my head.

Desire

I want a lazy, sad, and kinky kind of love.

November 3, 2016

I am a mess, and I want to be loved by someone as messed up as me. And I know that's messed up, but I want a love as chaotic as a hurricane that there would be nothing left in the end but glorious mess. And the need to start over again.

The Anatomy of My Heart.

1. Sadness
2. Anxiety
3. Hopeless Love

November 23, 2016

I need to fall in love with a hopeless romantic. Someone who would tell me that my eyes are like the stars at night and how my morning bed hair looks like a windswept forest that dances whenever the sky cries every time the ocean quenches her thirst for love. Someone who believes in fate, destiny, and magic. Someone who believes that finding true love is a necessity to cope up with the sadness and agony that life brings. Someone who believes that I exist.

Violet

I am waiting for you,
my blue moon, my cold summer,
my sad girl, my loveliest of all—
my half soul, and my half life.

The Girl I Love

My mother told me when I was young that there are two types of girls that will love me:

1. The girl who makes me happy but makes me feel unloved.
2. The girl who makes me sad but makes me feel loved.

She told me on rare occasions I'd find both qualities in one girl. But not every boy is lucky to find both qualities in one girl. So if I ever have to choose between the two, she told me, to always choose the girl who makes me happy because that's what she always wanted for me.

Yet I don't want a girl who makes me happy. I want a girl who makes me feel loved. So if I ever have to choose between the two, I will always choose the girl who makes me sad.

Ariel

She is the
View that
I keep seeing.

The dew
That flies
Every morning.

The girl
Only a few
Witness crying.

A new soul
Lies for her
Every evening.

If You Love Her

If you love her, you have to show her you love her. How? By showing her you need her. How you can't live without her. How? By dying for her again and again until you have her. Why? Because dying is suffering. And she's worth the suffering. Why? Because her love is worth the pain. And in her love—there is relief. And in her love—there is hope.

Princess December

She dances like autumn—
And she walks like rain.

She sings like summer—
And she talks like falling leaves.

That's why every time it snows in December—
I am rooted like the flowers at spring.

Perception of Reality

Reality is how I perceive it to be. How I can travel the world one day and watch snow fall in the Sahara. How I can dance in the rain and claim I am on fire. How I loved you all this time and claim I never was.

Sad Girl

Look at that sad girl.
She makes the clouds cry
because they have never seen
anything more beautiful than the sun.

November 26, 2016

It's so romantic to be loved by the girl whom I write poems to.

Observation

Loving you is not an obsession but rather an observation.

Accidents

I think we fell in love by accident, but I think there's no such thing as accidents. I only believe in the possibilities and probabilities given to us in this quantum universe. And out of seven billion people in this world I found you.

Atlantic

I lost my brain
somewhere while
I was swimming in
the deep blue sea of
my sadness searching for you.

All The Wrong Places

Since now I've found you, it's now your turn to find me in all the empty places I've been looking for you. And there you'll find every single piece of me still searching for you in all the wrong places.

Artists

She painted the moon
on my face while I painted
the sun on her face and I will
love her for all the days of our
lives even if the sun loses its rays.

Wanting

I want you to tell me that I am not enough for you. That every day you crave more of me. That I am a drug you are addicted to. That you thirst for the knowledge of who I am. My beliefs. My philosophies. My values. I want you to always expect for more because I have so many things to tell you—that a lifetime wouldn't be enough to express how much I feel better—now that I have you in my life.

Artisan

Where are the clouds today
and where is the color blue
all I can see whenever I look up is
the color gray and I want to paint
the clouds today with the color blue
so I grabbed the paintbrush of my mind
and opened the acrylic paint of my heart
and started painting words and I ended up
painting a goddess of my own.

The Story of My Life

I want to know the story of your life. From your oldest living memory to this point of time. I want to know everything that's inside that beautiful mind of yours. I want to know what makes it sad and what made it sad. I want to know what it is afraid of and what made it afraid of that. I want to know what makes it think about love and only love because I want you to be loved so I can begin to share with you the story of my life.

A Man of My Words

Words mean
so much to her,
so I need to be
a man of my own.

Storyteller

She was both fiction and words. That's what I loved about her. She wasn't just a story. She was a story that wrote stories. And I wanted to read her stories if only she would allow me to enter her heart again. And more than anything—I wanted her to write about me if only she would allow herself to write a sad ending to her happy story.

Souls

Let's swim in the sun when we're nothing but souls.

Well-Being

You are my okay when everything is not.

Every time I feel like everything in my life is falling apart, you are the roof that keeps me safe from the fallout that should've torn me apart. That's why I choose to live right beside you no matter what. A place beside your most beautiful part.

My heart beside your heart.

Human Sexuality

"Do you fall in love with boys or with girls?" I asked her.

"Sometimes boys," she replied. "Mostly souls."

Unconditional Love

By loving that someone without expecting to be loved in return is how you become a much more sweeter person.

Limbo

Somewhere between sadness and madness, I love you.

Madness

You told me life was madness. Filled with sadness.
That the only way to make it good was to find someone
with goodness. Filled with happiness. And that's why I was
surprised when you then told me you love me.

Fantasy

Love is a fantasy, but sometimes we need fantasy to fall in love.

Wonderland

We created a world where the sun rose in the evening, and the moon glowed in the morning. Where oceans replaced clouds. And our love replaced by madness.

Foundation

And sadness, when shared at its most vulnerable state, is the strongest foundation of a relationship.

Music

Listening to music with you under the stars is so wonderful. It's better than drugs or any self-destructive thing in the world.

Us

It makes me happy to be sad together with you.

December 18, 2016

Some nights we said nothing. Just listening to our silence. Just listening to the weird beat of our hearts because sometimes mine beats faster and sometimes yours beats faster. And I like it. Just you and me cuddling in bed. You are mine. And I am yours. And I am sure that if we can do absolutely nothing together aside from just simply being happy with breathing and existing together. Then I'm sure that nothing in this world can separate us from each other.

Purpose

Existing became living because of you.

Fool's Paradise

I gave her the kind of love that I read in books.
I wrote her letters. Took her to parks. Kept photographs
of her. Went to late night drives with her under the stars.
Fantasy was all I could really give her.

Follow The White Rabbit

Follow your heart.
Always follow your heart.
No matter how irrational or illogical it may sometimes be.
It will always lead you to lovely places that your mind doesn't know off.

Time's Paradox

There is a paradox in time when I'm with you. How a day spent with you feels like a minute. How a year spent with you feels like an hour. How a decade spent with you feels like a day. And how a second spent without you seems to measure forever.

Rabbit Hole

The only way out of the mind is being in love.

Chasing Bubbles

Falling in love with her was like being four years old again. Chasing bubbles, catching them, yet everything pops. And my hands would always be wet and empty with something that I have chased and destroyed.

Revolutions

Some revolutions happen in cities.
Some revolutions happen in my heart.
Some revolutions happen in my mind.
And every revolution ends with her skin on my skin.

Flightless Bird

You give me reason. So much reason to be alive today. You are my thing with feathers. You are the angel of my existence. You are all my reasons.

Atom

There's a part of me that feels only when I see you.

Venus

I look at her, and I see her.

She is so lovely to be in love with me.
She is so strong to be her becoming.
She is a strong she. She is a woman.

Every time she blinks a sea spits out a
thousand sunken ships.
Every time she breathes a dormant volcano awakens a
thousand souls.
Every time she smiles a whole colony reawakens after a
thousand millenniums.

She is worth a thousand years of revolutions.
She is worth a thousand tears of absolutions.

Absolute

I don't think that
I love you. I know that
I love you.

Comfort

I feel like I've fallen in love with the comfort that comes with you.

When someone asks me why you're my partner—I simply answer that you are the one that I'm comfortable with.

You're the one I don't have to impress because you have accepted all my flaws, all my imperfections.

And I feel that's how true love works. Being in love with comfort. Settling or not settling for your standards because the love of your life might be worse or better than your standards.

Love is not just a series of standards. Love is so much more magical than that.

Mood

Today, I am in the mood to melt under the sun with you.

Sunshine

If the sun laughed, it would resemble your warm smile.
Your smile replicates the same feeling
Of waking up with the sun on my face.

A feeling of subtle annoyance and joy
From the moment the sun kisses me half past seven.
Reminding me of a new morning, a new existence.

That's why every time I wake up with the sun on my face
I do not turn away. I do not open my eyes only to close
them back to sleep.

I just smile back just like how the moon smiles back
whenever the sun laughs at him.

Building Blocks

Your smiles; the building blocks of my happiness.

Your Smile

Your smile is one of those ordinary smiles that I get from random strangers that tells me to have a good day. But your smile is my favorite because when I see it, it just doesn't tell me to have a good day, it tells me to have a good life.

Orbs

Eyes are such divine living instruments that can make music out of any human being's soul without even touching it. Until it finally lets go.

Sunsets

We always watch the sunset from the shore.
We always watch it set from the white celestial clouds to the deep cold ocean blue. And sometimes I turn to you, and I see you smile as you slowly close your eyes. And I think to myself that you slowly closing your eyes could be as lovely as the sun dying.

Yellow

For you, I will live my life even if I feel like I don't matter every time I look at the stars.

Nightfall

And after a while, I noticed how the stars at night were intertwined in her curly blonde hair. And how the moon refused to leave her chest because it loved the sound of her heartbeat.

Superstar

I see the rings of Saturn in her eyes circles
I feel Jupiter's whispers blowing her Venus
painted hair as its beauty catches stardusts and
my universe will miss her when she goes supernova.

Star Shower

I don't know who she is tonight. She's beautifuler than she was yesterday. When the stars refused to cease when it rained.

Rainbow

I will follow the
end of the rainbow
if that's what it takes
for you to stop crying
and I will meet you there.

Pluviophile

You once told me how you loved it every time it rained. How you felt more confident to face the day from the moment you hear the raindrops falling from the early morning sky. How you felt more in the moment. How you felt more in love with me because you see the beauty in sadness whenever you danced with the rain.

Bromance

One of the best relationships in the world is when two males choose to treat each other like brothers and sometimes even like sisters.

Friendship

In my perspective, friendship is not really about playing hide and seek or finding hidden treasure chests for one week.

For me, friendship is more about being weak. It is about sharing each other's sufferings despite not finding any solutions to each other's mutual despairs. It is about being in a state of comfort in a life filled with grief and dejection.

For me, true friendship is found when a man chooses to jump off a bridge after another man does.

Humpty Dumpty

Falling in love with you is like
sitting on a brick wall. Just admiring
your beauty from a distance until I have a great fall.

Sometimes the pain that comes
from falling in love with you is better
than the pain that comes from not loving you at all.

Friendzone

I think she liked me in a way. Isn't that strange? Not being sure of a person's feelings for you. But I guess that was always the scenario with me and her. Full of uncertainty and maybes. The kind of relationship you see in couples who're not official but could be in the future with a little teaspoon of doubt. And it's hard. Being in love with a girl who only might think of you as a friend or a partner in crime or worse—a brother. But still. If she only sees me as a friend or a partner in crime or a brother—then I have no choice but to treat her the same and hope that someday—my love for her would evaporate like water dancing in the wind.

Broken things are made for better things.

The
Loss

How tragic
that the sea
separated us.

Azure

I've been wearing the sea
In my eyes lately.

And whenever I look at you—
I drown.

Memories

The sea.
That's not where I drown.

I Am Neptune

The god of sadness.
The god of melancholy.
The god of the sea that separated
you and me.

Spectrum

I don't know if you see the same blue whenever I wear the sea in my eyes. And I don't know if I see the same yellow whenever you wear the sun in your smile. But this—I place my hand on top of your chest—this is a spectrum. You are all the colors in my colorless world.

Puzzle Pieces

The world will break your heart
a thousand times.

And the people you love will break your heart
a hundred times harder.

And the person you love will break your heart
once and for all.

And that person will fix your heart forever.

I Am A Paradigm

I am a paradigm. I am an idea of someone else's love.
I am a belief that has been deeply rooted in someone else's
heart. And I want to be loved for who I want to be and
not whom I need to be in order to be loved by someone
who knows nothing about who I really am.

2000 Miles

"I'll never leave you," he said thousands and thousands of miles away.

Proximity

I am scared of falling in love with you because I can't see you because you're so far away from where I live. And I know that love is not and never was not about proximity but love is and always was something I wasn't sure of until I met you. And I am scared because I am now faced with great certainty that I don't know what to do but be subjected to self-doubt that maybe only in great proximity is where I'll fall in love with you. Because there I can't have you. Because there I can always love you without expecting you to love me back.

Refuge

Her scars are the places I call home.

Home

Home for me is not where I am. Home for me is a physical structure where the girl whom I love is sheltered and protected from the incoming storms of life. Home for me is not where I am safe, but where she is safe. Home for me is not where she exists, but where she lives. She is my home.

Support

I will always be ready for her sadness.

Fortress

It's distressing to love a girl who's been sexually abused. The feeling that no matter how secure I make her feel there'd always be this itch in my brain saying that I can never make her feel totally secure. That I'd spend my whole life as a fortress protecting a queendom that is already in ruins.

Suicidal Girl

The girl with the scars is the girl
I loved.

She who branded the stars in her wrists.
From her life filled with
wars, wars, wars.

That I couldn't stay and fly to Mars.

I Am A Paradox

I am a paradox. I love you, but I hate how much I love you. I tell you I'm happy, but I'm not. I'm willing to die for you, but I'm also willing to live for you.

Wanderess

She escaped the place where
she was free to do all things
to climb a tree like she was three.

Forever climbing and never looking
down with her eyes up the night sky—
never stopping until she reaches the stars.

Echoes

Even though I know that one day we'll cease to exist, and everything everyone does every day would be all for nothing once the sun finally explodes and turns us into stardusts—I would still be happy that I've shared my existence with you as I hope that one day we'll meet somewhere in the deepest voids of oblivion where we'll hear all the echoes of our love.

Monster

More than I want to
protect you from
the world.

I want to
protect you
from the monster

That I can be.

Beauty and the Beast

If you truly say you love me—come to my house in the middle of the night, and I will show you how I destroy myself, and how I am a monster disguised as a writer. And I will make love with you—if and only if you will love me in my most destructive self.

Deviant

I am half in love,
Half suicidal—

I am half calm,
Half anxious—
To fall in love again.

I am half full,
Half empty—
Without you.

Cicatrix

More than wounds I couldn't take any more scars. You make me feel unloved. And I don't know why that doesn't hurt me yet scars appear out of nowhere. Maybe I'm just sick of loving you. Maybe it's best to live the lonely life I once lived before I met you. Because there I'm the only one who can scar myself. And no one can stop me from scaring myself. Not even you.

Cheshire Girl

I fell
and fell
and fell
and fell

Down the rabbit hole.

Where I saw the world without time.
In a time when my capacity for self-destruction was out of
control.

And there I found her.
And there I saw her smile.
While she was sitting on a tree.
While she was gazing at the stars.

Falling hopelessly in love in Wonderland.
Where she told me was a place for crazy people.

And in that moment I knew that I was in love with her
sadness.
The kind of sadness that made her evaporate with her own
tears.
The kind of sadness that infatuated me to stay in a world
filled with madness.

Since every time she disappears, I lose parts of me.

Since every time she disappears, I find myself staring at the morning moon.

Hoping it'll turn blue because that's when she comes back.

And then I fall
and fall
and fall

Down the rabbit hole again.

Kissing her on a leafless tree—
under one blue morning moon
and a thousand giggling evening stars.

Curiosity

Curiosity never killed the cat; nor will love kill you.

The Gift of Love

It is not until you open the gift of love that love is realized.
Anything before that is just pure imagination.

Power Struggle

There's not a single relationship in the world that's without a power struggle.

Every relationship is a power struggle.

I Love You

I am yours. All yours. How much more vulnerable do I have to be for you to comprehend that? That I am willing to risk my life to keep you away from the danger of loving someone else. Because no one can love you better than me.

Variable

You always change.
Your love is inconsistent.
You are a variable in a sea of constants.

Someone

I hope that you will find someone like me in the future.
Someone who loved you in times of your sadness.

Alice

She was my Alice leaving my Wonderland,
and I wanted her to stay. I didn't want her
to wake up from a dream she was aware of.

I wanted her to be in love with the idea of me.
I wanted her to embrace the madness that comes
along with the process of loving me.

And I know she did embrace it. Otherwise,
she wouldn't have loved me. Otherwise,
she wouldn't have stayed.

The Most Tragic Thing

The most tragic thing in my life was making you the only anchor for managing my depression because I never thought you'd leave me.

Heavenly Friends

I have no friends.

But in the morning after I wake up I talk to the sun.
I tell her about you and how your love lights up my whole world.

I have no friends.

But at noon I talk to the clouds.
Asking them about conspiracies about storms, typhoons, and hurricanes.
Asking which one of them carried the most hydrogen.
Asking them what ozone layer is the best to live in.

I have no friends.

But in the afternoon I talk to the birds.
Asking them where they came from.
Asking them if they have a destination.
Asking them who their moms and dads are.

I have no friends.

But in the evening I talk to the moon.
I tell him about you and how your love lights up my whole world.
Especially when my whole world is dark.

Poetry

Every poem that I've created was yours. I thought they were mine, but they were yours. And I wish I could've kept them. And I wish I could've kept you.

You

Thinking of you heals me and destroys me.

You and I

Promise me we'll meet here in another life. You and I. This place where we first met and fell in love in this life. Promise me. We'll meet here. You and I. Promise me. Promise me we'll fall in love with each other again in another life. Promise me. You and I. Because one life is not enough for me to fall in love with you. Because one life is not enough for me to feel your love for me. Because one life is not enough for you and me. For you and I.

A Farewell Covenant

If you leave me on a hot summer day—
promise me you will take the sun away.

If you leave me on a humid spring afternoon—
promise me you will never love the moon.

If you leave me on a cold winter night—
promise me you will take the road that's bright.

If you leave me on a frosty morning fall—
promise me you will never love at all.

Growth

When both a girl and a boy finally lets go of each other because they know they're not meant for each other— that's a tragic moment for them. Millions of stars will die. Thousands of planets will sigh. Hundreds of shooting stars will ask lots of whys every time they pass by this planet. And a parallel universe will cry over the sad result in this universe.

But despite the dismay of the celestial wonders—mother nature will celebrate their loss like how flowers bloom in spring. Because mother nature knows that once a boy lets go of a girl, and a girl lets go of a boy—they'll eventually grow from their temporary sorrow.

That's the moment when a boy becomes a man, and a girl becomes a woman.

Nimbus

My clouds are becoming darker and darker.
I am beginning to lose touch with the dark sun.

Goodbye

It felt to me like her wounds were out of this world that neither love nor time could heal. And I would never understand such suffering.

Little did he know he was going to be okay.

The
Self-Love

If I do not love myself, then I should not love at all.

The Philosophy of Self-Love

Your ability to love other people comes from your ability to love yourself.

The key to loving yourself is knowing that you are enough today. That you are able to accept yourself no matter how dark you feel your life is at this very moment. That your hope and inner peace lies in accepting yourself as who you are at this very moment, forever changed.

Life is too short for you to live a life filled with regrets and what ifs. You must have the power to look at yourself in the mirror every morning and say: *I am forever changed.* Because every day you are forever changed. You are a forever work in progress.

That feeling lost in life is how you find yourself.
That it's okay not to feel okay sometimes because that's how you grow.

That it's okay to rest when you're tired because working in fumes would only eventually lead to self-hatred and burnout.

That setting yourself on fire by self-endangerment is not shining but rather burning. That self-care, self-love, and a well-balanced life are the only ways to truly shine.

That you are beautiful.
Not beautiful like everyone but beautiful like you.

That you are art long before anyone painted their love on you. That you are music long before anyone sang your beautiful name. That you are poetry long before anyone pressed poems into your lips.

That finding good, meaningful, and enjoyable work is important in learning how to love yourself because without work life has less meaning.

That you are like the sun, and you were always born to shine. That you are like the moon that gives light to the world in times of darkness. That you are like the rain that helps other people grow in times of drought.

That you have plenty of time to love others in this life of yours, please learn to love yourself first.

Love Yourself

It isn't guaranteed that if you love yourself others will love you back. But love yourself anyway.

Dear You

It's okay to give up on something you do not love.
Just quit. The universe is an unlimited supply of love.
Because without love, there is no purpose. And without
purpose, there is no life.

Passion

Do what you love.
Whatever it may be.
And let it destroy you.
And let it forever recreate you.

The Greatest Love

Your love for yourself in times of your sadness is the greatest love of all.

The Greatest Healer

Do not forsake your sadness for it is the greatest healer of all.

Cumulus

It's crazy how I'm still alive after turning into a storm a couple of days ago. And I'm still breathing. And I'm still feeling. And I know that I am like a cloud that absorbs sadness from this world so easily but right now at this very moment I am okay. I am a cumulus cloud. And I will endure my future storms for moments like this.

Thought Cloud

Sitting here on top of
the clouds of all my foggy
thoughts and philosophies
there is a question that's as
tall as a mountain:

What if you still love me?

The Sky Is Empty

Sometimes I look at the sky
and think
of the possibilities
of you still loving me
even if I know, you don't.

Superior

Sometimes hope is more powerful than love.

House

Her body carries
depression and anxiety.

No wonder she let go of me.

Monsters

When you left me, you left your monsters with me, and I am starting to love them and call them my own.

Forgiveness

There is love in forgiveness without reconciliation. The point of forgiveness is not for you to forget the past mistakes of those who've wronged you. The point of forgiveness is for you to move on and love yourself and move towards the wonderful possibilities that are waiting for you in the future.

Stasis

I have both feminine and masculine energy inside me.
Both are so equally powerful.

I'm

I am beautiful.
I am handsome.
I am a human being.
I am wanted. I am loved.

I am love in times of hate.
I am hope in times of despair.
I am alive in times of destruction.

I am peace in times of distress.
I am faith in times of disbelief.

I am. I am. I am.

I Am Beautiful

Yes.
Yes, I have the power.
To be this sad and this beautiful.

Pimples

I gazed at my face in the mirror this morning, and I saw a cluster of stars—old and new that were imperfectly placed in the galaxy of my own reflection. Some of them placed near each other, and some of them dead, and some of them were about to create a supernova in the near future. But most of them have already passed away—leaving black holes to suck the happiness out of my own universe. But what I have learned since the big bang was that a universe without planets and stars is a universe without beauty. And loving the galaxy of my own imperfections would be the greatest joy of my life.

The Love You Deserve

You deserve a love that's deeper than the ocean.
A love that's brighter than the sun.
A love that's higher than the mountains.
A love that you can only find inside yourself.

Self-Love

In my stormy sea of pessimism, there is a small boat of hope that never capsizes. Searching for love. Searching for me.

Euphoria

Sometimes I laugh out
of tragedy because life
gets worse and the only
way to cope up with it is
to make a comedy
out of it.

Narcissism

I am sometimes in between narcissism and self-love whenever my depression is sometimes replaced with euphoria. And I am still trying to love myself in the most healthiest way possible without feeling like some sort of minor god whenever the sun obliterates my darkest of clouds. Because there really is a huge line between narcissism and self-love. And in my blue brain where the sun seldom shines through my darkest of clouds—it could really be a hard task not to feel too overly excited about the slightest amounts of happiness.

Bliss

I find bliss in accepting the fact that the sun does not
shine forever in my world.

Happy Things

I think I should write more happy things. Focus on the good things that I have rather on the good things that I think I want. Focus on the self-love that is rather than the unrequited love that was. Focus more on writing just for myself. Focus more on writing whenever I am happy.

Always

Sunrise is the start of something beautiful: the day.
Sunset is the start of something beautiful: the night.

Happiness

Good books. Good foods. Good eyesight.
Good digestion. Watching the sun rise. Watching the sun set. Watching the stars twinkle at night. Finding Venus in a cluster of stars. Losing track of time while playing video games with my best friend. Seeing my mother smile back at my father's smile. Seeing my brother sing at church.

It's the simple things really.

Siblings

"There are just some things that you are too young to understand." Life said.

"But I never want to grow up!" Love replied.
"I want to stay young forever!"

Stardust

I am made from the same dust that allows shooting stars to fly. I am made of fire and light to burn brightly in this dark universe. My origin is unknown. I am still light years away from my search for the truth. The meaning of everything. The meaning of life. I am going to touch it one day. I am going to touch it one day, and every single thing that made me feel less than who I already am would make sense. I am going to keep it. I am going to treasure it. I am going to believe in it. I am going to allow myself to fly.

Youth

I want to grow without feeling old because there is so much more to learn and love with so little youth.

Wendy

You loved him, but he was made of pixie dust. And you were afraid to fly with him because you didn't believe that he loved you.

Time

Time is the intangible object that is felt
through love and hate
through hope and faith.

It is the seed that makes these things melt
as we learn to grow and wait.

Peter Pan

Sometimes I feel like I am Peter Pan stuck in Neverland. Refusing to grow up. Acting like I am still ten years old when in fact I am almost twenty. Doing the childish things that distract me to avoid the anxiety of being subjected to the real world where people grow old. And by refusing to grow up, I am deluded into thinking that I am always one step closer to immortality.

Tinkerbell

Teach me how to fly.

Pixie from Neverland.

I never want to grow old
and bold
and cold—

As now I need a hand
to hold.

You innocent little thing—

Sprinkle your pixie dust
all over me!

Those sparkling things full of
gold
you hold.

Teach me how to fly.

Pixie from Neverland.

Teach me how to fly.

Up.
Up.
Up.

In the sky,
up high—
till we die!

As I want to learn how to
grow old with you—

You pile of gold
I sold.

Decay

How wonderful it would be to meet myself one day
beneath the flowers.

Sad Wonderland

I want to chase butterflies forever in this sad wonderland of mine. I never dug to discover gold but to discover who I am down this rabbit hole. But I'm afraid that even the most extreme dreamers like me would eventually succumb to reality where we'll get our illusions destroyed.

Dreamer

I dreamed, I believed, I conquered.

I Am A Believer

I am a strong believer that fate exists. That everything happens for a reason. That the people we have in our lives are in our lives without accident. There is always meaning. Explainable or unexplainable. There is no such thing as luck. We are all here for a purpose. All we have to do is believe.

Pure Imagination

Do you sometimes think that if you believe in something with all your heart and soul it would come true? Simply by pure imagination.

Rome

I want to live in a world where people don't practice abortion but rather contraception. A world where people are in love with rather souls and not genders. A world where everyone is free to worship any god. A world where women and men are treated equally politically, economically, and geographically. A world where women are protected from rape rather than being blamed for rape—marital or non-marital—both are obviously equal. A world where criminals are brought to justice not by means of death but by means of hope as they learn new things to become a better person while in jail. A world where a person's mental health problems are nothing to be ashamed of. A world where every human being's story is heard. These are the things I imagine whenever I dream of a better world.

The Beauty In My Stars

"Too much imagination. Too much creativity. That's why dreamers don't succeed in the real world." they told me.

"I know," I replied. "But in all the worlds I've created I was free—and I was alive—and I was loved. And I still am."

The Bigger Picture

I know that a forest is made up of individual trees, but when I look at a forest, all I see is a forest. And that's pretty much the same when it comes to my outlook in life. I just look at the bigger picture and summarize everything I see with pure feeling and intuition. Because I learned that when I try to make sense with tiny details of information—it kills me. And it's really a challenge for me to live in a world filled with so much logic and explanation that it kills my own morals and perspectives in life—which gives life for me less meaning and beauty whenever I am faced with its harsh realities. Because sometimes I forget that bad things happen in this world whenever I think of it as a place filled with love and beauty.

Freedom

The things we love owns us, but they're the things that make us free.

Correlation

Love is not constantly reciprocal. Not everyone you love will love you back. And not everyone who loves you will be loved by you. But one day someone will love you back. And you will love them back again. Because on that day, love is constantly reciprocated.

Depression (Noun)

Another word for healing.
Another word for self-love.
Another word for hope.
Another word for life.

Words

Love is not an emotion. It is a four lettered word. How we feel it is based on our relationship to that word to many words. Like depression. It is a ten lettered word. It means severe sadness. An emotion. But my relationship to that word is synonymous with many words. Like love. Like healing. Like hope. Like living.

Blossom

To shine is not to burn but to glow.

Metamorphosis

You changed because the pain pushed you to.

Sow

Plant seeds in
the broken places
of your heart.

You don't want
weeds growing
out from it.

Altruistic

For you to choose to fill the empty parts
of yourself on your own rather than to let
someone do it for you is very selfless
of you.

Baby Steps

My growth as a person does not have to be perfect.
Any kind of growth is powerful.

In This Moment

In this moment, I am alive. I am healthy. I am free to create things with love. The pain has already passed away. And if it does return—I will survive. I will see pain not as a weakness but as an opportunity to rest. To resharpen my saw. To remember to do things lightly to improve the quality of my work. To remember that over exhausting myself would only lead to not just feeling tired but feeling fatigued and burned out. A feeling that I've always felt before in a time when I thought doing things in fumes was a sign of hard work and taking things lightly was a sign of laziness.

So in this moment, I am reminding myself to care for myself. To always take one step back every time I move two steps forward to evaluate if what I am doing is with love and meaning.

And in this moment, I am hoping you'd consider doing the same. I am hoping that you'd give self-care and self-love a chance before diving into the things you do in life. And in everything you do I hope you always remember to always dream as you also live in the moment.

And lastly and most importantly, I hope you always remember that in everything you do always be gentle with yourself. Always do things lightly.

Belief

To hope is the only way one can do the impossible.
But if one falls and fails, it is also only hope that makes it
possible for one to stand up again.

I Am A Flower

I believe I can make it because I am near the finish line.
I believe I can do it because I am almost done. And
I believe that someone out there above the stars loves me.
A guardian angel or a god or an entity that never stopped
believing in me when it was so hard for me to believe in
myself. Especially when I stopped believing in myself. And
whoever you are, someone or something from
somewhere. Thank you. Thank you for watering me. For
teaching me to believe in myself in times of nimbus clouds
and brutal storms. In times when it is hard for me to
believe in myself.

Sprout

Evolve and never stop growing.
Choose excellence over perfection.
Always in all ways trust the process.
And never ever stop believing in yourself.

Bloom

I love the moment when a flower grows out from the rocks where it doesn't have that many nutrient to support its beauty, and yet it still lives.

I Am Rooted

You can cut me from my stem, but my beauty would always remain in my roots.

I Am A Gardener

I will always cry my way out of life. Tossing random seeds of sadness in every corner of this world. Watering them with my tears until the whole world sees the beauty of healing that comes out from sadness. And let those who are know that they're not alone. That self-love comes out from sadness. That self-love is a lifelong process.

Green

Your body is your own forest, you could chop or grow as plenty of trees as you please.

November 18, 2016

Dear Self,

You should focus more on watering your own grass
rather than on looking at other people's greener grass.

I don't want envy to be your primary source of motivation
on doing better in your craft but rather your love for your
craft to be your primary source of motivation.

Sometimes it's not the color of the grass that makes
us who we are but rather the feeling of being a gardener.

Love always,
Self

Solicitude

Show great
solicitude to
yourself by
finding joy
in your solitude.

Vulnerable

Who told you that falling in love vulnerably is a curse? Believe me when I say that it is not a curse to fall in love vulnerably—it is a gift. Every day I fall in love vulnerably with people who don't love me back. Every day I fall in love vulnerably with flowers and trees. And every night I fall in love vulnerably with the stars. And every time I dream—it's always about me falling in love vulnerably with myself.

I Look At Her And We Are Still Together

Our daughter still has the color of your eyes and
the shape of your nose while she still has the color
of my skin and also the size of my mouth and both
of our broken hearts in one.

A Letter To My Future Daughter

I'll have you one day, and I'll love you with every inch of my soul. I'll let you be whatever you want to be as long as you're safe and happy. I'll write poems about how you're the greatest gift that I could ever have in my life, and I won't embarrass you in front of your friends. I just want you to be free. I just want you to experience the happiness that I haven't that much experienced in this existence of mine and seeing you happy, seeing you smile on sunny days will be the greatest hope on my rainy days because even though you don't exist yet, daddy loves you so much, and daddy is doing his best to stay alive because he knows that you're worth living for. You're worth the sadness. You're worth all the sorrow just to hold you one day in his arms, as he sees a beautiful human being filled with love. As he sees his entire universe in his arms. And he wouldn't miss that for the world.

Offspring

I am Solitude.
Loneliness is my mother,
and Serenity is my father.

Through The Looking Glass

I am legion. I am a saint when it comes to my parents. I am a bitch when it comes to my brothers and sisters. I am a mute when it comes to strangers. And I speak in tongues when it comes to my friends. Especially when I am under the influence of alcohol. And to society? I am a ghost. But what intrigues me the most is my identity when it comes to my own self. Who am I exactly? Am I just an actor? A performer? Or do I become more like myself when I act? When I perform the roles I want certain people to believe in? Who am I exactly? I am nobody. I am perfect.

Lovechild

I am the lovechild of sadness and comfort.

Family

My father is good in math and logic. He's an engineer.
My mother is good in health and love. She's a nurse.

Maybe I've adopted their talents.
Maybe I'm good in multiplying love with my words.
Maybe I'm a writer.

Truth

There are more winters in life
Than summers.

There are more autumns in love
Than springs.

Sunrises

I hope you realize that every day is a fresh start for you. That every sunrise is a new chapter in your life waiting to be written.

Nicknames

My name is always June
when people first get to know me.

I am kind.
I am warm.
I am flowery.
I am summer.

I am always good at first impressions.
I am always bad at keeping those good impressions.

My name then becomes October
when people then think they know who I am.

I am the person they view as cold
because I begin to isolate myself from them
because I begin to annihilate myself from them
because I begin to become who I was and who I am.

My name is December
and nobody knows who I am.

I am also kind
but I can be a ghost at times.

I am not that warm
but I can be a person's calm.

I am not that flowery
but I can be a person's truth.

I am winter.

I am always good at starting all over again.
I am always bad at ending to start all over again.

Colour

Maybe that's why the sky is blue.
For us to see the beauty in sadness.

Paradox

I am a child with an old soul. I see magic in everything, but at the same time, everything tires me because I feel everything so very deeply.

December 19, 2016

The sky is blue today.

Not that bright but not too dark. Just gloomy enough to make me feel hopeful as I look up and see a thousand feathers at the sky. It reminds me of all the things that makes me who I am. Melancholic. Peaceful. Poetic. Beautiful. Lonely. Lovely. Blissful.

I feel pure serenity splashing inside me like calm ocean waves because today I am part of the sky. I am one with the sky. I am one with nature because I am a beautiful human being. I am nature because I am alive because I choose to be alive. I am forever changed.

Suddenly I feel flowers sprout out my brain as the sun nearly sets from a distance. It's beautiful. Just like my brain. And today I am a cumulus cloud.

I run towards the setting sun as I think of everything I can do with my life.

Write. Read. Travel. Meet new people. Learn new skills. Sing. Dance. Laugh. Cry. Smile. Take a selfie. Eat. Exercise. Find someone to love. Love myself. Love my family. Love my friends. Love my dog. Take my dog for a walk in a park. Say hello to people in parks. Tell them my life story.

Share more about my story through poetry.
Inspire people to share their story. Write more.
Read more. Learn more. Love more. Inspire more.
Believe in myself more. Live.

Author's Note

Hello. Thank you for reading my debut poetry collection. You make me feel so happy.

I created this book of poetry to showcase my love for writing and self-expression and to let anyone who read this book know that mental illness is real and to let anyone who has it know that they're not alone and that there is always hope.

www.save.org

Acknowledgements

Thank you, mommy, for always being there to love me and care for me in the darkest times of my depressions. You will always be the brightest star that gives me hope every time I turn into a dark universe of melancholy.

Thank you, Ryan, my bestest friend in the world for encouraging me to live when I felt suicidal and bringing me out to the world when I felt too depressed to go out of the house. I think without you the world would be a much more horrible place for me to live.

Thank you, Renzo, for creating the wonderful cover for this book. You are always a very talented and reliable person. I am blessed to have a friend like you in this crazy world.

And last but never the least, thank you so much for my loyal readers on Tumblr, Wordpress, and other social medias for liking, sharing, and reacting to my writings. Every single one of you gave me strength to finish this book. Every single one of you gave me strength to live.

Please leave at least a short review at your place of purchase and if possible at least a short review as well at goodreads. It would help me so much. Thank you. ✿

About The Author

Juansen Dizon is a boy with clinical depression who discovered his love for writing after he dropped out of college early 2016.

He also loves to read, blog and love everything that gives him hope to live.

Confessions of a Wallflower, published at age nineteen, is his first poetry collection.

More of his writings can be viewed @ juansendizon.tumblr.com

About The Book

Confessions of a Wallflower is a collection of poetry, prose, quotes, and personal journals about depression, self-love, love, loss, and healing. It's a journey to pain, sorrow, and suffering where the only destination is hope.

Made in the USA
Middletown, DE
07 October 2018